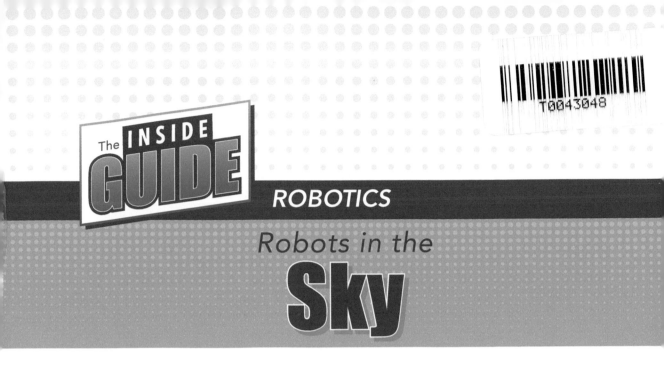

The INSIDE GUIDE

ROBOTICS

Robots in the
Sky

By Leonard Clasky

Cavendish
Square

New York

Library of Congress Cataloging-in-Publication Data
Names: Clasky, Leonard, author.
Title: Robots in the sky / Leonard Clasky.
Description: New York : Cavendish Square Publishing, 2022. | Series: The inside guide: robotics | Includes index.
Identifiers: LCCN 2020023258 | ISBN 9781502660527 (library binding) | ISBN 9781502660503 (paperback) | ISBN 9781502660510 (set) | ISBN 9781502660534 (ebook)
Subjects: LCSH: Drone aircraft–Juvenile literature. | Robotics–Juvenile literature.
Classification: LCC TL685.35 .C53 2022 | DDC 629.133/39–dc23
LC record available at https://lccn.loc.gov/2020023258

Editor: Caitie McAneney
Copyeditor: Abby Young
Designer: Deanna Paternostro

Find us on

CONTENTS

Robots in factories are often bulky and stay in place, which makes them very different from lightweight flying robots.

Robots are amazing machines that can make our lives easier, safer, and even a little more fun. These mechanical devices are built to perform tasks, and people can control robots or program them to work on their own. Some robots are **stationary**, but others are built for the sky!

What Is a Robot?

Robots were first developed to replace workers in factories. Today, factories still use robots to make products, but other robots save lives during emergencies or perform dangerous jobs, like search and rescue or military operations.

Every robot is different because each is made for a specific task. Whatever robots might look like or whatever jobs they may do, though, most share the same basic components, or parts. Basic parts of a robot include the sensors, frame, motors, effectors, and controller. Even robots built to fly have these components.

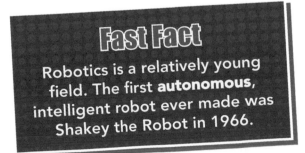

Fast Fact

Robotics is a relatively young field. The first **autonomous**, intelligent robot ever made was Shakey the Robot in 1966.

Drone Designs

Flying robots are also known as drones, or unmanned aerial vehicles (UAVs). People who design and build drones have to keep in mind what job the drone has to carry out. For that reason, there are many different drone designs, from military drones that look like airplanes to a simple quadcopter. All drones, however, have the same basic parts.

Sensors are the parts of a robot that gather information about the robot's surroundings. Some robots have cameras and microphones that act like eyes and ears.

The frame of a robot keeps all the important parts together and gives it a specific shape. Effectors are tools that help a robot perform a task, like picking something up. Motors, called actuators, drive the action of a robot. For flying robots, you need a motor for each rotor, or spinning blade.

The final basic component of a flying robot is the flight controller. Some drones are preprogrammed, while others are controlled remotely by a person on the ground.

Fast Fact
The Predator was a well-known RPAS used during the U.S. war in Afghanistan in the early 2000s.

Quadcopters are used for many jobs. They can record images for the news, help law enforcement, and some are just for fun!

How Does It Fly?

Anything that flies needs to abide by certain scientific laws. There are four basic principles of flight that people need to keep in mind as they're designing and building drones: lift, thrust, drag, and weight.

First, the drone needs lift, which gets the robot into the air. Lift is the upward force acting on an object. The rotors act as a fan, pushing air down and causing the air to then push up on the rotor, lifting the drone vertically.

Fast Fact

Quadcopters have four rotors, so they need four motors.

The controller acts as a robot's brain, guiding it to complete certain tasks. If you have a robot's remote control, you have the power to move the robot.

To go forward or backward, left or right, a drone must spin the correct rotors in the correct direction to tilt the frame and thrust the drone where the flight controller wants it to go.

Drones also need thrust, or the force that moves an object in a given direction. Faster rotor speed increases thrust, which can cause a drone to climb, or ascend. Slower rotor speed decreases thrust, which causes the drone to drop, or descend.

Drones need to overcome drag, or the force that acts upon a body in the opposite direction of the body's movement. People who build drones, called engineers, also have to keep weight in mind because the weight of the drone determines how much power is needed for lift and thrust.

ROBOTS INSPIRED BY NATURE

Nature is an inspiration for many robotics engineers. How do bees and dragonflies fly so well? Many flying insects and birds are much faster and more **maneuverable** than drones, so engineers study their flight mechanics. This helps engineers to improve their drones.

Engineers have developed tiny robots called microdrones, and some of them are based on insects. Some of these tiny robots have flexible bodies and flapping wings, and they can fit in tiny spaces, zip around corners, and avoid **obstacles**. In fact, engineers developed a microdrone inspired by a predatory wasp that can open doors 40 times its weight. Microdrones may one day be used to help in disaster zones.

The next time you see an insect fly, observe the mechanics that make its flight possible and successful.

Using robots, such as package-delivery drones, is often cheaper than employing people for the same tasks. This is good for companies and consumers, but it often puts people out of work.

Many drones are built to do a job, and today, engineers are finding more and more ways to employ flying robots. Some drones are already doing important jobs today, while other tasks are still a dream for the future. Developing working drones is one way that technology is making life easier.

Aerial Photography

Some drones are used for taking photographs and videos from the sky, also known as aerial footage. People can mount a camera on a drone and record what's happening from up above.

Aerial footage is improving all the time, but it isn't a new field. During World War I (1914–1918) and World War II (1939–1945), aerial photography from hot-air balloons and airplanes was used for reconnaissance, or finding information about an enemy. The first commercial aerial photography company was formed in 1919. Early aerial photography was used for surveying and mapmaking purposes. Soon, the growing motion picture

Fast Fact

The use of drones in filmmaking became legal in 2014. Drones have been used in major films like the *Jurassic World* movies.

Some drones are used for personal photography, including wedding photography. They allow overhead and wide angles that wouldn't be available with regular cameras.

industry started to use aerial video cameras. Helicopters equipped with video cameras are a common sight on the sets of many movies, television shows, and commercials. Over time, drones became a safer and sometimes cheaper option for aerial photography and filming.

Search and Rescue

Search and rescue operations are incredibly risky, especially in disaster areas or enemy territory in a war. Luckily, drones can help!

Drones can help find people after a natural disaster such as an earthquake or hurricane. These robots can be sent into an area immediately after the disaster instead of waiting for it to be safe for human rescuers. Some drones are used to deliver food and medical supplies to people who are trapped in hard-to-reach places.

Drones were used during and after Hurricane Harvey in Houston, Texas, in 2017. They can spot survivors, deliver ropes and life jackets, and check on power lines.

NEWS DRONES

Hollywood isn't the only user of drones for aerial photography. **News media** outlets around the world often require aerial footage for

their reports. News outlets often use helicopters for aerial footage and traffic reports. However, drones can provide a cheaper and safer alternative to news helicopters, getting closer to the action and providing more detailed images. Drones can even provide detailed video of traffic accidents and high-speed car chases. In recent years, drones have been used to provide eye-in-the-sky coverage of large-scale protests and other major world events. They can also provide detailed footage of natural disasters without endangering reporters.

This drone pilot is capturing aerial photography for the news.

In 2018, Ghana approved the deployment of drones to deliver lifesaving medical supplies and blood to people in need.

Drones can also help find someone who is lost in the wilderness. Equipped with cameras and even night vision, these flying robots can search an area of land in a fraction of the time it would take a human search party. Law enforcement agencies and military branches can also use drones to find escaped prisoners or enemy targets in dangerous areas.

The Future of Delivery

Someday, you might order something online and have it show up at your

Fast Fact

A special sensor on drones can detect body heat, so it's easy to use drones to find a person or animal in the wilderness. This is called thermal imaging.

doorstep soon after, dropped off by a drone! This no-contact delivery can help in times of disaster or disease or when important medical and food supplies are needed in a hard-to-reach area. Delivery drones are built to use **GPS** technology to find the correct address for delivery.

In 2019, the UPS Flight Forward program was the first to gain approval from the **Federal Aviation Administration (FAA)** for a for-profit drone delivery system. Other delivery companies and online retailers, such as FedEx and Amazon, are developing technology and seeking legal certifications, or approval, for drone delivery systems. Because of U.S. laws and rules for aircraft, it might be a while still before drone delivery is the norm.

Someday, packages from Amazon might be delivered by drone to your house!

Drones can show extreme sports up close! Camera drones can record close, real-time footage of snowboarders, such as those shown here.

Chapter Three

FUN WITH DRONES

Like other types of robots, drones can perform big jobs in some of the most important industries in the world. However, sometimes drones are made just for fun or entertainment. They can enhance the experiences of people visiting theme parks or going to concerts, and they can even compete in a sport all their own!

Drone Racing

Flying a drone can be more than just a hobby—it can also be part of the competitive sport of drone racing. Drone racing involves pilots flying quadcopter drones through difficult courses at high speeds, sometimes up to 120 miles (193 kilometers) per hour!

Fast Fact

The biggest competition for drone racers is the World Drone Prix. The first World Drone Prix took place in Dubai, United Arab Emirates, in 2016. The winner was 15-year-old Luke Bannister from England.

Skilled drone pilots can compete in the Drone Racing League. Pilots use special drones mounted with cameras that allow first-person view (FPV) through goggles worn on their heads. The pilots use the livestream camera to control their drones as they fly through

Drone racing involves small quadcopters with mounted cameras that allow pilots to see the courses the drones are flying through.

challenging courses. Races are broadcast on major sports networks, including NBC Sports, and on social media platforms such as Twitter.

The Newest Attractions

People visit theme parks and amusement parks to be entertained and sometimes even dazzled by new technology. Robots and machines play a large part in some theme park experiences, from rides to **animatronic** creatures. Drones may be the next big attraction at theme parks around the world!

Disneyland introduced its first show featuring robots that moved and made noise in 1963. Since then, these robots have been stars of the Disney theme parks!

Some amusement parks, such as SeaWorld in San Diego, California, have developed plans for nightly aerial drone shows. Using hundreds of mini drones, they would look somewhat like fireworks shows. The drones would form various shapes and movements in the sky, all set to music. Since traditional fireworks can be damaging to the natural **environment**, drones could be a more sustainable solution.

Drones have also been used at Disney theme parks and the Wizarding World of Harry Potter at

Fast Fact

The FAA granted Disney permission to use small drones over their theme parks in 2016. Disney put on a holiday drone show that year at Disney Springs.

Drones can be used in place of fireworks, or alongside them, to put on a high-tech show.

DRONES AT THE OLYMPICS

The Opening Ceremony of the Olympics is a chance for the host country to show off both old traditions and new technologies. The 2018 Winter Olympics took place in Pyeongchang, South Korea, and the Opening Ceremony featured very special performers—drones!

The brilliant light show used 1,218 drones—the most ever used for such a purpose—to create patterns from Olympic rings to an animated snowboarder. This was a feat of engineering and coding, and also a work of art. The Shooting Star platform, created by Intel, allowed the drones to move in perfect patterns, making the impressive show possible.

Intel produced the drones used in the 2018 Winter Olympics, showcasing the newest autonomous drone technology.

Universal Studios. Dennis Speigel, president of International Theme Park Services, said, "You're going to see them used throughout the entire entertainment industry, at football

These drones put on a light show to celebrate the 2019 South Asian Games in Nepal.

games, basketball games, stadiums, everywhere. In the industry, we're excited about it."

Drones in Concert

Canadian rapper Drake excited his concert audiences in 2018 when he used drones as part of his performance. These miniature drones acted as "backup dancers," preprogrammed by drone **choreographers** with a set routine to enhance Drake's show. The drones helped create a kind of magical experience for the audience because the technology was being used in a new way.

The drones, created by autonomous drone makers Verity Studios, are sure to be used in more concerts in the future. Superstars Celine Dion, Lady Gaga, and Metallica have also used microdrones in their musical performances in recent years.

Fast Fact

Lady Gaga used around 300 drones from Intel's Shooting Star platform in her 2017 Super Bowl halftime show. They flew in many formations, eventually forming an American flag.

Even if you buy a ready-made drone, there are still plenty of things you need to learn about to be able to fly it.

Chapter Four

FLY YOUR OWN DRONE!

Drones aren't just fun to look at or read about. You can fly your own drone! You can either buy a drone that's already put together, or you can build your own. Pay attention to local drone laws, and always put safety first.

Build Your Own Drone

If you want to build your own drone, where can you start? First, you need to decide what kind you'd like to build. A tricopter has three motors, a quadcopter has four motors, a hexacoptor has six motors, and an octocopter has eight motors. The most popular design is a quadcopter.

Next, research, or look up, the different parts that your drone will need. If you're building a quadcopter, you'll need a frame, four motors, four rotors (or propellers), a battery (usually a lithium polymer battery), a flight controller (with a paired remote control), and sometimes electronic speed controllers (ESCs).

Fast Fact

There are two types of motors for your drone: brushed and brushless. Most cheaper drone kits come with brushed motors, which have a simpler electric input component.

As with all robots, building a drone from scratch can give you a deep understanding of how it works.

Finally, personalize your drone. If you want to use your drone to take photographs or record videos, you'll need to add a camera. Add LED lights to fly your drone at night. You can even decorate your drone with special parts and stickers.

Now that you've built your drone, what happens if it doesn't work? Make sure to go back through the directions from your drone kit or instructional guide. Make any adjustments, and test your drone again. Engineering can be a trial-and-error process!

Drone Safety

Drones can be very fun, but they can also be dangerous. It's important to get familiar with drone safety before you start to fly your drone.

The FAA is in charge of keeping our skies safe, and it makes rules and regulations for most flying objects, from airplanes to personal drones. The FAA has certain rules for registering drones. If your drone is more than 0.55 pound (0.25 kilogram), you have to register it with the FAA.

An open field like this one is a great place to practice flying a drone.

Some quadcopters are very small. If your drone is under 0.55 pound (0.25 kg), you don't have to register it with the FAA.

Make sure you fly your drone responsibly. Choose a safe location, far from crowded public places or airports. You might want to record footage of a sports game or concert, but flying over crowds like that can be unsafe and sometimes illegal. Keep your drone within 400 feet (121.9 meters) of the ground. Safe places for flying drones include empty parks, big backyards, or empty fields. It's important to know your local laws about drones because different places have different rules and regulations.

Flying into the Future

Imagine a drone dropping off pizza at your front door. Imagine a light show made up of tiny flying drones. Imagine a world where drones can

PRACTICE MAKES PERFECT!

Practice flying your drone in a wide-open space. Work on basic maneuvers, or movements, first. To start, you'll want to practice ascending (going up), descending (going down), and hovering (staying in one place in the air).

It's also important to learn the language of flight, especially the terms "roll," "pitch," and "yaw." Roll is the rotation of a drone along an **axis** from front to back, which makes it lean left or right. Pitch is the rotation of a drone along an axis from left to right, which makes it lean forward or back. Yaw is the twisting of your drone in place. You can use these three flight maneuvers to move your drone through the air.

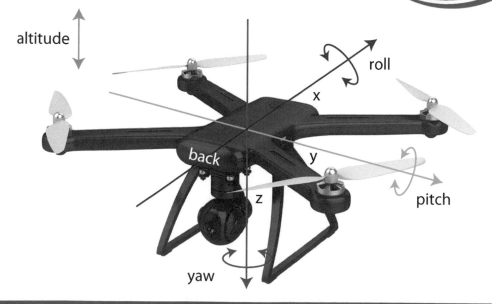

Aircraft like drones move along three different axes—front to back, left to right, and up and down. This diagram shows how the terms "roll," "pitch," and "yaw" relate to these directions.

altitude

roll

x

back

y

z

pitch

yaw

What would you order by drone? Food, medicine, and important supplies might be the first drone deliveries, but there are many possibilities for the future.

save lives during natural disasters and pandemics, or times when a sickness spreads around the world. The technology to make all this possible already exists!

Flying robots may redefine the future of sports viewing, delivery systems, and live entertainment. You can be a part of the future of robotics by learning about and building your own drones. With the right tools and knowledge, the sky's the limit!

Flying drones together might be a fun activity for your family to try.

THINK ABOUT IT!

1. Think about how drones are used in the military and law enforcement. How do they help people? How could they hurt people?

2. Think about filming a movie using drone photography. What kinds of new angles could you capture? What kinds of landscapes or cityscapes would you show?

3. Microdrones may someday be used in place of fireworks. How else could drones be used in entertainment?

4. Imagine you have a fleet of delivery drones that can fly long distances. How could you use them to fulfill a need in the world or help someone?

GLOSSARY

animatronic: Of, relating to, or being a puppet or similar figure that moves by means of electronic devices.

autonomous: Able to carry out a task without outside control.

axis: A straight line about which a body or a geometric figure rotates.

choreographer: Someone who arranges or directs the movements, progress, or details of something, often a performance or dance.

deployment: The sending out of something to be used for a specific purpose.

environment: The natural world around us.

Federal Aviation Administration (FAA): The part of the United States government that regulates civilian air traffic over the country.

GPS: Stands for Global Positioning System. A system that uses satellite signals to locate places on Earth.

maneuverable: Able to be moved easily while in motion.

news media: Sources and presentation of news and information, such as TV, radio, newspapers, magazines, and internet articles.

obstacle: Something that makes it difficult to complete an action.

stationary: Not moving.

surveillance: Close watch kept over someone or something.

FIND OUT MORE

Books

Conley, Kate. *Inside Drones*. Minneapolis, MN: Abdo Publishing, 2019.

Scott, Mairghread. *Science Comics: Robots and Drones*. New York, NY: First Second Books, 2018.

White-Thomson, Stephen. *Drones*. London, UK: Franklin Watts, 2019.

Websites

The Drone Racing League
thedroneracingleague.com
Step into the world of drone sports with the Drone Racing League!

5 Drone Safety Tips for Your Family
www.familyeducation.com/entertainment-activities/5-drone-safety-tips-your-family
Learn important drone safety tips on this website.

Know Before You Fly
knowbeforeyoufly.org
Know Before You Fly is an educational campaign to help drone users—from professional pilots to recreational flyers—learn how to safely fly their aircraft.

INDEX